The Dominant Wife Series

Submissive Husband Fantasies – "And there I was…"

By Mistress Jessica

ISBN-13:
978-1719178310

ISBN-10:
1719178313

First Edition

This book is for entertainment purposes only

The idea is that with good communication between partners, healthy role playing can be obtained by both parties consenting and agreeing on each role they will play during this time. As with anything respect for both partners is adamant and expected by all involved. Safe words and Safe Gestures should always be employed to ensure that the submissive person has a way regardless of the situation to be able to communicate with the dominant person, these and all ground rules should be set up prior to any role playing of any kind.

You and only you are responsible for your actions.

Have fun, but play safe!

~Mistress Jessica~

Introduction

I love submissive men, in fact I keep a few around the house just to amuse me. Now that may not be something you are into and that is ok. The fact that there are many men who would give anything to be involved in a Female Led Relationship or as people like to call it these days (FLR) gives the world a little hope.

This book is an outlet for me and the continuation of the Dominant Wife Series of books. If you are into this type of stuff then check out our other books in this series.

Dominant Wife Rulebook

Dominant Wife Rulebook – Chastity Edition

Both have received some good feedback.

Let's face it I have a dirty mind and one of the things I like to do is write short stories, they really get me turned on while I am writing them, which is probably why they are short stories, because I usually have to get one of my own submissive men from around the house to come over and finish me off after just a few pages.

I am sure some of you can relate to that.

I hope you enjoy these short stories as much as I do.

Feel free to email me for any reason I love to hear from my readers - mistressjessica01@gmail.com

And there I was…

Home from work and I knew something was amiss in the house, there was no noise, everything was quiet. I didn't see my wife Julie anywhere about.

"Julie are you home" nothing but silence.

My office door was ajar, I pushed it completely open and to my astonishment found my wife sitting at my desk, looking at my computer and some very extreme kinky pornography, in fact the pornography that I was looking at the night before and had obviously not cleared my browser history.

"Is this what you like? Is this what you look at when you touch yourself?" she asked.

I had lost the ability to speak.

It never really dawned on me what would happen if Julie knew the kinky sex fantasies that I dreamed of and could only see online.

Her tone was one of strength and it kind of turned me on a little. I had nowhere to go with this; I figured my best response would be to tell her the truth.

"Yes" I began.

"Videos of women dominating men really turn me one." I told her.

She sat back and looked me up and down.

"What about this Sissy, Chastity, and Cream Pie stuff? Is this what you want?"

I dropped my head gave the matter some thought, I now felt like I was jumping into a rabbit hole. I nodded my head and heard her take a sharp intake of breath in astonishment, and I could feel her glare.

She got up from my desk and angrily left the room slamming the door behind her.

Needless to say there was not much talking after that, we ate in silence and afterwards, she went to bed and told me to sleep in the guest room. Saturday morning came and as I made my way downstairs for some coffee Julie was already having her cup.

I started to say something but she stopped me raising her hand indicating for me to wait. She took another sip of her coffee cup and proceeded.

"Dan I truly love you and will do anything including those things I saw in the video. In fact I think I would very much like to help you out with this little fetish of yours." She told me.

As you can imagine, I was ecstatic to hear those words and also at the same time a little scared to think my wife would be willing to do those things to me.   I was going to try and back pedal a little bit but simply accepted that she would be in control now.

The first thing she had me do was to shave all my body hair off, it took a little while and a couple of razors but I got the job done, she even helped me with my back, my skin tingled like it had electricity sizzling across it.

 "Oh my god you look so pretty" She said

She admired my smooth crotch and my hard cock; she ran her fingers up my leg to my ball sack which she took firmly in her hand. I hadn't expected her to lower herself but she was excited at the beginnings of my transformation.

Julie took my cock into her mouth and began to suck me slowly and gently, her fingers were soon off my balls and one was making its way up and into my ass, then a second and third. I could feel her nose touching my skin, as she began to move her fingers in and out of my asshole; I wasn't going to be able hold on to this when she pulled her fingers out and released my cock from throat and my orgasm was denied.

"Let us get some things straight before we go on from here" she said.

"I am fully in charge of you, you will do what I say when I say it, and if you don't you will be punished. Now get over there and lay face down on the bed." She told me.

I was very excited to see this side of my wife and didn't hesitate to move my hairless body to the bed an assumed the position as she indicated.

"One of the things you need to know right away as we start this new chapter in our lives is if I am angry you will feel pain, and if I am happy you will feel pleasure. Right now I am angry that you hid this part of yourself from me for such a long time and as such you are going to be punished." She told me

I could see in her hand that she had one of those thin canes and I knew this was going to be very painful to endure. As she began I felt a wave of pain flow through my body I didn't even bother to keep count as she rained blows down upon my bare buttocks. Soon the tears were flowing freely from my eyes and she was crying to but for different reasons. When she finally stopped and she ran her hand across my butt the welts were raised high and red and my sobbing continued.

"Are you still happy that I said yes" she asked me.

Between the sniffles and sobs and tears I looked up at her.

"Yes I am" I said.

She smiled.

And there I was

I heard the click of the lock, in that one split second from the start of the sound to the end of the sound I saw clearly for the first time of what I had done, it was too late to put a stop to it, and now I was in her control.

"Now you belong to me" She whispered in my ear.

A few flashes later and a full accounting of what she had done to me was now fully documented and in her possession. I was painted into a corner and with no exit I was forced to give up control to her, of everything, and that everything included the right to touch my own cock.

It was now kept behind a layer of plastic that I could see it but would not be able to touch it.

"There will be a few changes around here" she said.

"From now one you will be the one to do the housework while I get to do whatever I feel like." She continued.

"Look I even purchased a maids uniform for you and you will wear it whenever you are at home." She told me.

She threw the maid outfit on the bed, it was one of the standard black and white ones, with the fishnet stockings.

"Get changed and meet me downstairs." She said.

I looked at it for a moment and realizing my dilemma I began to put it on. I had to admit the fishnet stockings felt very good and this seemed to cause another problem as my cock was responding and trying to get hard but there was no room for it to grow, the pain was terrible as I tried to think of non-sexy things which was hard as I was standing in this sexy maids outfit slipping on high heels that she left made the outfit complete.

I was not used to the heels and didn't want to break my ankle going down the stairs so it took a little while but I finally made it to the main floor of the house.

One of my buddies must have arrived while I was changing and he looked at me and then at my wife like saying WTF.

"Don't mind the new maid, with my husband gone and who knows when or if he will ever return I am going to need a good fucking so I figured I would start with his friends first." She told him.

My friend looked at me again and then at my wife like he wasn't sure what he should do, like he was caught in some sort of domestic argument and he didn't know whose side he should take.

She was only wearing a robe and when she let it fall my friend and buddy didn't glance a second time at me he was too entranced by the naked body of my wife, I had to admit so was I but any chances of me getting a hard one were carefully locked away.

When my buddy or who I thought was my buddy moved over and began to kiss my wife and run his hands up and down her body fondling her breasts and they were nice and expensive breasts I should know I paid for them.

It didn't take long before she was undressing him and when those pants came down she got a good look at his cock.

"Your cock is so much bigger then my husband's cock." She told him.

Just watching her touch it and hold it made my own cock strain against the cage that it was in and it hurt.

She fondled his cock and it grew even bigger, she would look at me as she held his cock and then she took into her mouth and began to suck it, which wasn't easy as he was big. When she was satisfied in her humiliation of me she stood up and told him to fuck her.

He bent her over the couch so that I could see very clearly from where I was standing, and right before he put it inside of her; she turned to him and said.

"I want you to fuck me in my ass, I need your big dick to fill me up, it was something I wouldn't let my husband do because his cock was too small, will you do that for me." She said seductively.

My buddy didn't even look at me.

"If you need a big cock in your ass then I am more than happy to supply that for you" he told her

He spread her cheeks and spit on her ass a few times to get her wet and then he began to work his cock into her, oh she screamed as he opened her asshole first in pain and then in pleasure and her rode her ass hard.

I could see her hand between her own legs as she rubbed her clit as this monster went in and out of her asshole the moaning turned to screaming and the puddle on the floor under her crotch said it all as she called out to god and her whole body shook from the orgasm the rolled in and around her body.

He filled her ass up with his load and then withdrew his spent cock.

She looked at me like everything that just happened was my fault and it sure felt like my fault but at the same time my cock was pushing against the cage it was in like a monster trying to escape.

He sat on the couch as my wife stayed in place motioning for me and then pointing at her ass which was covered in cum

"Get your mouth over here and clean me up" she ordered me.

I scurried over to her like the good little maid and got down on my knees as she pulled her cheeks apart and licked my buddy's cum right off her gaping asshole.

"Now stick your tongue inside me" she told me.

I did as she instructed and was rewarded with a large amount of cum that I had missed.

"I hope you like your new duties as the maid because I am going to be fucking your buddy a lot." She told me.

My buddy still looked confused about the whole thing and though he also looked incredibly satisfied after fucking my wife.

He looked at me finishing up licking his cum up from her ass and then at her.

"I think my husband may be gone for good" she told him.

He nodded in agreement to her and told me to come over and clean his cock with my mouth too.

And there I was

Putting away the laundry for my wife one day, she had to run out to the store, I don't remember what for. It wasn't a really big deal, I mean I had put the laundry away before, we used to do it together, it was fun and romantic, or at least it became that way once we started flirting with each other.

Today though it was all me, and after my own socks and boxers were put away all that was left was her under things. She did buy the beautiful panties, they were so soft and silky, I never really noticed that before, I guess I was usually more interested in getting them off of her beautiful heart shaped ass so I could sting her with my hard cock.

Not sure why I started to pay attention more to the way they felt against my own skin as I brought them to my face and gently caressed my cheek with a pair. I kind of got lost in the moment and I felt my growing cock in my shorts, and it wasn't long before my shorts were down around my ankles and my wife's panties were wrapped around my cock. The feeling was amazing, I never had done something like this before, and now I was thinking to myself this was a most exquisite feeling. I looked down at my very hard cock wrapped in her panties and a wash of shame and humiliation came over me quite suddenly, this wasn't what a grown man should be doing. All of a sudden I heard the garage door opening, there was no time to change, I pulled on my jeans over the panties as my wife walked in.

She must have seen my hard cock through my jeans and immediately came up and started rubbing it through my pants. I tried to move away but evidently she was pretty horny herself and her hand was sliding up and down my shaft as she kissed me and the feeling of her fingers and the silky material of her panties my cock was in ecstasy. She kept whispering in my ear how much of a big man I was and that my manly cock was so hard as her hand moved faster it didn't take very long before I was shooting a load of hot cum which leaked through the a panties and made a big wet spot on the front of my jeans.

"Well someone must have been horny today, whatever brought that on you should be doing all the time" she smiled at me.

"Now without your big cock how am I going to get my pretty pussy satisfied." She asked me

The adrenaline from it all was still racing through my body as I pushed her down on the bed and reaching up beneath her skirt and pulled her own panties off and sniffed them as they were damp with her scent. Raising her legs I began to reciprocate the pleasure as I used my tongue on her beautiful smooth and glistening pussy.   I made her cum more than once with my tongue before her body was tingling and untouchable as she would jump at the slightest touch.

I had forgotten all about her panties in my pants so when I dropped my pants to change them her cum filled panties fell right on the bed in front of her.

"What is this big fella, have you been wearing my panties." She asked with an evil grin.

"No I wouldn't do that" I stuttered an stammered.

"It is ok if you do, I kind of think it is sexy actually, they are all silky and satiny your cock would look great in panties" she told me

She got sat up on the bed and touched my soft cock.

"Why don't we do a little test" she said.

I had no idea what she was referring to but she picked up the panties she had been wearing and held them out for me to step into, which I did without even thinking about it.

They were satin and had pretty bows on them and as she brought them up my legs closer to my cock and balls I could feel the heat within me growing as well.

When they were in place she didn't waste any time but began caressing my cock through them and in about a minute I could feel myself getting hard.

"Well look at that I guess you are a panty boy after all" she smiled

I had misgivings about the whole idea at first, it sounded like she was making fun of me and then she took my cock out of the panties and began to suck on it.   It had been quite a long time since I was able to get hard so soon after cumming.

"If you are going to be my panty boy then I want to be your dirty slut, so take your hard cock and put it in my asshole" she told me.

This caught me off guard as we had talked about it but we had never done it before, I took some lubricant we keep in the end table and put some on my cock and her asshole.

"Come on panty boy, fuck your dirty slut of a wife" she said aggressively.

I pressed the head of my cock against her asshole and slowly pushed into her, her fingers were all over her clit as pulled out and pushed in a little deeper and then again.

"Oh my god, that feels so good" she told me.

I pushed further until I was fully inside of her, she became like an animal.

"Fuck me hard you little panty boy, do my panties feel good on you, fuck your wife's ass come on give it to me hard"

I started really fucking her hard and with that and her rubbing her pussy she began to squirt which was something new for both of us and I couldn't hold back anymore and came a second time deep inside of her ass.

We both lay there spent on the bed

"Wow" I said.

"You aren't kidding either" she responded.

"Well I guess that is settled then" she told me.

I looked at her with a raised eyebrow

"I am throwing out all your underwear and you will be wearing panties full time from now, no if's and's or but's about it." She told me.

We both laughed at that.

The next day my underwear draw was empty except for a pair of her panties and a note.

"Went shopping I wasn't kidding about the panties"

"PS this is just the beginning"

It made me wonder what other things of hers I could enjoy wearing.

And there I was…

On my back with my wife's pussy right above my face, her lips were wrapped around my cock, and her best friend Sally's husband push his huge cock into her from behind. You may ask how did I get into such a predicament, well I guess I should start at the beginning.

We had been drinking and playing some stupid board game, soon we were drinking more than we were playing the game.

"No way, you are joking with me, you will have to prove it to me" I heard my wife say to Sally.

Well needless to say Sally proved my wife was wrong as she deftly opened her husband's pants and withdrew a rather large cock. He just looked at me and shrugged his shoulders as if this thing happens all the time. I felt a twinge in my own groin as I watched my wife reach out and she touched it. Said something to sally about how smooth it was and then her hand was wrapped around the shaft of it.

"Oh honey is this okay with you? Do you have any problems with it?" She asked me.

He gave me that look like this really did happen all the time. I shook my head that indicating I was ok with whatever she wanted to do. His cock had increased in size since the last look I had given it. With my wife's hands still on his cock Sally took the head of her husband's cock into her mouth, it looked like my wife was feeding it to her; I had to admit it looked hot.

My wife had the look of desire in her face, and she wanted that big cock inside of her.

This brings us to my current predicament.

His cock was slick; her lips glistened as they hugged his shaft. He was stretching her and she was enjoying it, over and over again I could feel her legs shaking as she pushed back against him. The moaning of her throat felt good on my own cock except that she kept stopping to ride each climax he was giving her.

I would be careful and lick her clit when his cock was not in my way I wanted to be respectful after all I wasn't into guys but every once and awhile his thrusting would often put my tongue more on the shaft of his cock rather than my wife's clitoris.

All this time Sally had been very quiet about the whole thing, here her husband was fucking my wife and I couldn't even see what Sally was doing.

I soon found out what Sally was doing during all of this, evidently she had her own agenda and ideas of what she liked to do when her husband was fucking another woman. I felt her bring my legs up in the air, I had figured she was going to take over for my wife on my cock, I thought this will be nice two women sucking my cock, it was almost worth letting my wife get fucked by another man to have this experience. Then Sally slid her finger into my ass I felt a little weird but it kind of felt good while my cock was being sucked. The next thing I felt was not her finger.

Evidently Sally wasn't just sitting on the couch being quiet she was quietly getting herself ready by putting on her strap-on harness which evidently she carries around with her in her purse for just such occasions as this. I am sure if I looked at her husband he would have given me that look you know the one that says, this happens all the time.

The head of the strap-on was much larger than her finger, and she wasn't too concerned about my comfort as she pushed it in, I think I may have screamed like a girl right there and then but luckily everyone was too caught up in the moment to realize.

My wife then stopped sucking my cock, I guess she was watching what Sally was doing to me.

On Sally's next push I felt her thighs on my buttocks; and she was all the way in. The pain reasonated through my body it reminded me of a brain freeze feeling when though this pain was emanating up my body from my asshole. Sally not having any compassion for my situation simple pulled herself out of me and pushed herself back into me. She soon was thrusting into me at the same speed as her husband was entering my wife; it was a most surreal moment to see.

It wasn't long after that, the pain seemed to ease away and was replaced with what could only be described as pleasure, first it was just a small pleasure but soon she was rubbing up against my prostrate with her hard plastic cock and a different type of pleasure began to well inside of me.

I raised my head and began flicking my tongue on my wife's clitoris and that took her to a brand new place and she began screaming with pleasure at which point she took my cock back into her mouth which felt amazing, so amazing I began to shoot my load noticing how amazing it felt with this plastic cock up my ass.

I rode that orgasm for all it was worth, my whole body tingled with the electricity of the moment it was exquisite.

With my own spent cock sliding out of my wife's mouth cum still dribbling out of it, Sally didn't seem to pay it any mind as she continued to fuck me harder and harder, evidently her strap-on had another piece on her side that was entering her each time she thrust into me, so to get herself off she had to really fuck me hard, and she rode my ass until it was sore from the beating it got with that plastic cock going in and out of it. Eventually she came which only left the big guy as my wife must have already cum a number of times.

You would think they would have switched positions and let me up but he kept pumping away at her until he was ready and when he was my wife was singing the high notes as he filled her pussy up to over flowing.

Of course I didn't even think about it when he pulled his spent cock out of her and fell straight down onto my face and my open mouth, it was covered in cum. Globs of his cum were just dripping from her well fucked pussy and falling all over my face. My wife turned around and proceeded to push all of the cum on my face into my waiting mouth. His cock soft was still very big, but I opened my mouth so I could suck on the head of his cock then gave him a look like yeah this happens all the time.

And there I was…

Clothes shopping, it was such a terribly boring experience for a man, you have the choice of jeans or dress pants, and you get to choose between blue, black, or brown. It was so utterly depressing; the average men's department in any department store is about one quarter the size of the women's department.

The stigma of being a man even walking through the women's department is so strong within us it is like trying to breakthrough a strong obstacle course within our mind.

I started to look at the types of clothing that we offer our different genders; it seems so goal oriented, on the men's side of things you have strong hardy clothing meant to protect to keep safe to guard against injury and wear. When I looked at what was available in the women's department I didn't see any of those things. Everything seemed like it was geared towards being vulnerable, being delicate, even being fragile and needing protection. It was an amazing thing to come to the conclusion that we dressed so differently.

I wanted to experience something of the delicate something of being vulnerable and with that I found myself touching and feeling the material of a very pretty pink panty. I pulled my hand away as if someone was watching me and thinking I was some sort of pervert for touching a pair of women's underwear.   I found my hand drifting back to it to feel its softness its delicateness and I thought to myself that I just had to have it.

At this point my mind was racing as I held this pair of panties on its little hanger and made my way to the cashier. I felt as if every person was looking at me and that they knew that I was buying this pair of panties for myself and that I was not a real man because a real man wouldn't wear women's underwear now would they.

Waiting in line to make my purchase I heard a girl giggling and I immediately turned around to defend myself and my manliness when I realized she was not giggling at the pink panties in my hand but some other matter that had her attention. The mother of the girl gave me a curious inquisitive look at my panties and then myself, but said nothing and moved her attention to her giggling child.

The cashier picked up my panties and in a large voice told me how pretty these would look on me, and that they had matching bra's on sale as well. I started to blush and she continued I bet you would look real pretty in pair of stockings as well, why don't you take these back to the ladies department and I will have someone come over and help you to pick out a few more things.

When the store speaker came on and a lady named Sally was told to come up to register six that she had a new Sissy that needed some help in finding his way through the ladies department. I could see everyone looking at me and giggling and laughing and I was embarrassed and really turned on at the same time.

With my face beet red I was ready to drop the panties and run out of the store. Before I had a chance to do any of those things there was a very nicely dressed woman in front of me with the name tag that read SALLY.

Please come with me sir.

I could still hear everyone giggling and snickering behind my back

Sally though was a strong minded woman and she told me not to pay attention to those people that they had no right to judge me and the things that I wanted to wear.

Sally held my arm and took me deep into the women's clothing section. I felt like I had never been this far into the woman's section at all, I was seeing things I had never seen before.

We went right to the fitting section and she measured me as best she could and then she told me to disrobe.

I told her I just wanted to buy a pair of panties.

She wouldn't have it though and explained that I could either disrobe or she could forcibly remove the clothing from me.

Now I was scared more of Sally then I ever was of buying a pair of panties.

Needless to say I disrobed in front of Sally

She measured me up and down back and forth, there seemed to be people coming and going though they all kind of looked like a blur like they we were somehow separate from the rest of the world.

It seemed like I closed my eyes for a second and when I opened them I was fully dressed as a girl, an then I would drift off and when I came around I was dressed differently though still as a girl.

It seemed like whatever Sally was doing was taking forever, but at the same time it felt like only a moment ago I was up at the cashier.

When I finally woke up fully Sally was there and we were walking back out of the woman's section and I was still holding those panties I so much wanted to buy.

The cashier was there and when I handed the panties to her to pay for them, she told me how pretty I would look in them and how they would match the bra and stockings I was wearing.

Nobody giggled behind me or laughed it was like they were not even paying attention to this man buying woman's underwear for himself.

I reached into my purse and gave her the money I had to admire how pretty my pink finger nails looked and even took a moment before she gave me the receipt to freshen up my lipstick.

"Have a wonderful day" she told me as I walked away with my high heels clicking on the floor tiles.

And there I was…

I had been tied up spread eagle on the bed by my girlfriend who went out on her date and left me like this suffer. I was just glad that only she saw the bra and panty set along with the stockings and cock cage which she had me put on and were just there to add to the humiliation of it all.

Why did I let her do this to me, I should stand up for myself, be a real man. Of course we knew deep down inside that I wasn't a real man and that I liked this attention from her.

"Honey I am home from a night out dancing and drinking" She yelled as she walked into the apartment.

There were two other voices in the house and I didn't recognize them. She had brought two people back from her night out. I could only hope that she would keep them out in the living room and that she wouldn't let me be seen this way.

Nope there they were all three of them my girlfriend and two guys and they had their hands all over her body and down her panties and under her bra. She broke away from them and removed even those pieces of clothing until she climbed up on top of me naked face to face.

I could hear the two guys taking off their own clothes making some comments about the state of myself all locked up and dressed like a girl. This seemed to turn my girlfriend on even more.

"His cock is huge" she said to me.

"I made sure of that before we left the club" she said looking into my eyes.

Then she moaned and I could tell his huge cock had entered her and she forgot all about her little sissy boyfriend tied to the bed.

Soon She began to moan and dig her nails into my chest and his penetration continued deeper and faster, she was already spun up from being out and it wasn't long before she was climaxing, and two more climaxes after that and he shot his load inside of her. That was when she turned herself around on top of me and began to suck the cock of the second guy with her.

"Time for you to do your part now boyfriend" she told me over her shoulder with the guys cock going in and out of her mouth.

She scooted back and placed her cum filled pussy upon my lips and with my tongue out I received my prize. She knew how I liked to suck cum out of her pussy and she was always so accommodating when she would go out for a night out on her own to make sure she thought of me laying tied up in her bed dress all pretty with my cock locked up tight. I could no longer see her but I could hear her giving it all she had with this guy's cock, and as I made her climax with my tongue deep inside of her cum filled and well used pussy I heard her moan deeply. Guess that was the last straw and the vibrations sent him over the top he pumped his load down my girlfriend's throat.

There was some pleasantries and they asked a few questions about me and she easily deflected about this is what we are into; they seemed to accept it for what it was worth.

"Thanks again boys hope to see you out dancing next time." She told them and I heard the door close.

"Well look at you did you have fun tonight while I was out" she asked, and I nodded.

"God wasn't his cock so big I may have to bring him home again, maybe next time I will let you be the one he fucks." She giggled and I imagined what that would be like.

"Now since you were such a good boy and licked all of his cum out of my pussy" she said.

"Maybe you deserve a reward" she continued.

She opened the drawer and rummaged around and came out with a small key, then she unlocked my cock cage, and my dick sprang to life.

Her hand was gentle yet firm, with a little lotion she would get me close and then stop and then get me close then stop.

The teasing was incredible.

Then she sat across my legs and used my hard cock to rub her clit, never letting me enter her just going up and down, I was almost there and she was concentrating on her own coming climax and wasn't paying attention to me, I must of made a sound or something for she stopped, and finished herself off with her vibrator.

"Wasn't all that fun, you almost snuck an orgasm in for yourself, guess you will be more quiet next time when you are close" she laughed.

With some ice from her drink and few good slaps on my ball sack, my cock was brought back down to size and locked back up. The key was removed from the room to a new hiding place and I was released from my bounds and with a kiss on the lips she asked me to snuggle, she told me how she likes the feeling of my plastic cage pressing up against her ass cheeks.

And there I was…

Tied up tight couldn't move a muscle, I felt the rope tighten as she finished the last of the knots.

"There you should be secure enough now. How are you feeling my pretty little husband?"

Replying was useless as the gag in my mouth prevented any response.

This evening's game was the sissy husband, yes I was tied up tight and couldn't move a muscle but just prior to that I was over her knees as she paddled me with the wooden hairbrush, of course she had to raise my pretty skirt and pull down my panties so that the handle would strike my exposed baby smooth butt. She had hit me pretty hard with the brush and I still had the welts to show for it.

She finally removed the gag but I was immobilized still and now she was giggling as she began applying lipstick to my lips, probably bright red that is usually her preference I wouldn't know until I saw the pictures.

Click. Click. Click.

"These will look so good up on the website sweetheart."

She enjoyed humiliating me this way. I couldn't see anything and that afforded me a little respite since with the mask my face wasn't easily seen.

"I have something special for you tonight my dear"

If I was correct I would be worshiping her strap on next.

"Open up your mouth sweetie time for you to show how much you have learned."

The next thing I felt was not her strap on. It took a moment or two to realize that what was in my mouth was an actual cock of another man. It was soft but from the warmth of my mouth I was making another man excited and this strangers cock was filling up my mouth. It was much thicker and was touching the back of my throat.

Click. Click. Click.

Now she had pictures of me with a real dick in my mouth this was not going well.

This stranger was now moving his cock in and out slowly.

"Oh sweetie you look so hot with your red lips all over his cock. Isn't this what you wanted to be a real girl, well real girls have to suck cock so let me see you enjoy sucking his cock."

Without even giving it a thought I began to suck on it, to raise my head so I could take his cock deeper into my throat.

It was one of my darkest desires how could she have known, but she had and there I was sucking off a stranger. I used my tongue on his shaft when he pulled it from my lips. He held it so I could lick the head of it, which was very big.

Click. Click. Click.

I was glad no one could recognize me with this girl mask on my face, and back into my mouth came his member. I was used to sucking on strap-ons as my wife made me learn to take large plastic cocks deep and I was doing it now and I could tell this man liked it. His hands were holding me still with his cock deep in me, he withdrew suddenly I knew he was going to cum all over my mask.

It was then that my wife pulled the mask off of my face as his hot cum sprayed all over my face in my eyes, on my nose and all over my lips where the head of his cock came to rest on my open mouth and just as another load dripped into my waiting mouth.

Click. Click. Click.

The flash was in my eyes and the cum was on my face. There was no way for me to live this one down, in about a half hour she would have these pictures up on the website where they would be copied and transferred all over the world.

I knew eventually someone in the company would see them and my life would take a change.

But for right now it was pure heaven as I took the initiative and took his cock back into my mouth and see if we could get him to cum again.

And there I was…

I was thinking of about my wife putting me into a chastity device.

At the last dinner party I was at, my best friend had announced to us that his cock was locked up by order of his wife Emily. She had found him cheating on her, and she took him to court and the court found that she had certain rights to John's genitalia.

We all laughed and thought it was a big joke until Emily told us it was true and told him to show everyone, which evidently was also her right given to her by the court. The next thing I knew we were all looking at my friends locked up cock.

When we were alone, I asked him about it and how it worked; he didn't hesitate but told me I better be careful, the laws were changing fast and if I wasn't careful I would find myself in a cage. I was sort of fascinated by it, his cock was surrounded in what appeared to be plastic of some sort. It was perfectly fitting his cock, they had air holes and a place for him to pee out of but other than that it was hands off no touching going on here.

Two weeks later at the office the Manager had to announce to everyone that his wife had locked his cock up. He didn't drop trousers but there were a few girls in the office that seemed happy that the manager's cock was locked up. I had heard later he had been making unwanted advances on some of the girls in the office and they had spoken to his wife about it who took him to court right away and took care of the matter by putting his cock in a cage.

Then it was in the news about case after case of men losing the rights to their cock and balls. The papers were having a field day with it famous actors stepping forward some even displaying the chastity device proudly for all to see.

I was devilishly excited about these devices; I mean to have the woman I truly love controlling my cock and balls seemed like one of the most erotic fantasies ever. Knowing that she would have the power to release me and let me cum and feel pleasure. Every time I thought about the idea of it my cock would be rock hard for hours.

It was about that time I began seeing my hopes for something similar to happen to me to fall apart, it was obvious that I was not being very promiscuous, in fact I had even been caught wearing my wife's panties at the office one day, the secretaries never let me lived that down. I think my wife may have told them I had them on just to embarrass me, because they seemed to know that I had got caught touching myself and she was punishing me for it.

At one point I had to simply ask why she hadn't done to me what everyone was doing to their husbands, I was actually jealous of these other men who could no longer touch themselves, but only when their wives wanted them to.

My wife still refused to do this for me, she kept telling me that if she did it would not be as the others were and that I probably wouldn't like the fact of how it would turn out.

I didn't understand what she was talking about and kept pushing the matter of how I wanted to be like the others.

So here I find myself in the ante chamber of the court house, my wife did finally take me to court but she had insisted that I lose the rights to my genitals because she had found them to be unfulfilling.

I was so embarrassed to hear her testify how I was unable to give her a proper orgasm.

So I became the laughing stock as my cock was locked up for being inadequate, I hadn't even bothered to find out that in my circumstances the wife after proving her husband's inadequacies did not have the control to release her husband that in fact the lock that was used did not have a key as removal was not allowed.

Furthermore my wife was given a legal right to be promiscuous in finding her sexual gratification so now I would come home from work and find some strange guy fucking her in our bed and only when she reached orgasm was I allowed to enter the room.

In fact the only way that we eventually found that I was allowed to orgasm was when she used her strap-on and only through anal sex could I achieve orgasm, after that she made sure I knew what a big cock felt like and from the pool of cum on the bed when she was done I knew I had found something to truly love about her again.

And there I was…

In the dark, I had a butt plug up my ass, it was uncomfortable just sitting in the chair, the panties I had on didn't offer any respite, they just pulled the chastity cage downward so that my rapidly hardening cock was in that much more agony.

The one thing that did give me a little comfort was the stockings, it always came down to that, you could have some cheap skirt on but when you wore good stockings it made you feel like a million bucks.

The fake breasts my wife had gotten me for father's day were big and heavy and after she glued them to my chest I began to have a new appreciation for women with big tits, of course they looked fucking fantastic in the push up bra I had on.

That was when she slid the dildo gag into place and shut the closet door.

I was fully encased in blackness of the closet or so I thought.

My hands were tied behind my back and my fee to the chair, the fact that I was in five inch heels didn't mean I couldn't look good while being totally submissive and humiliated.

My cock strained at the cage my balls ached from the hard plastic ring around them, but I was able to touch my knees together and with a little motion I could feel the wonderful expensive hosiery I had on and felt aroused even more.

It was about then that I noticed the light.

She had actually left the door open a crack and I could see out directly onto our bed.

I was pretty sure she did that on purpose just so I could see what was to happen next.

There was a noise and my wife entered into the room and it was one of my buddies from the poker game downstairs. She had told them I ran out to the store before she put me in this predicament, and now I knew why.

Steve was tall man good looking and me and the boys had more than once mentioned the size of his cock jokingly on a poker night or two, I guess she wanted to find out for herself.

I was glad to see Steve was hesitant about the idea but she wasn't going to take no for an answer and she had his cock out of his pants and in her hot little hands, and then it was in her hot little mouth.

I watched the whole thing in amazement as she took it deep into her throat with still more to go she wasn't going to waste any time and the short blow job was over and it was time for Steve to earn his prize.

She laid back down on the edge of the bed and her legs in her very sexy stockings were raised up above her head and she simply told him to fuck her like there was no tomorrow.

Steve pulled back so he could get his cock lined up and he slid that puppy in all the way to the hilt, the deeper he went the louder the moan, and out it came and this time he slammed that thing home, he began to fuck her in earnest. I saw the wet spot on my pretty panties appear and then start to grow I was going to be leaking big time.

Steve was a powerful man and he demonstrated that power as he was being very rough with her, as he rode her like a jack hammer, she responded to his hammering away with lustful sounds of orgasm after orgasm.

I must have gotten a little too excited and accidently nudged the door with my shoe, it started to swing open, I couldn't do anything about it, when it was half way open Steve turned and saw me and looked at the way I was dressed.

His comment to her was simply how poker night just got more interesting.

He called the rest of the group up and showed them me and told them that my wife was now fair game once a week; my wife just looked at me and smiled.

Steve came over and got real close, my eyes must of show sheer terror in them. He whispered don't you worry little lady my dick will be hard again in about twenty minutes and I can give you a ride just like I did your little honey over there.

The wet spot got a whole lot bigger right then and there.

Then each one of my friends took turns with my wife, and nobody noticed Steve slide my chair into the next room and close the door.

I guess it was my turn with Steve now.

And there I was

The moment I felt the cool liquid touch my skin and felt her fingers wrap around the shaft of my cock, I knew the session was over and I would be going back into the cage. The feelings of ecstasy still rolling up my spine, as well as the pangs of frustration knowing once again she was not going to let me have an orgasm.

"Not this time Henry, you know what I said earlier. You will be allowed to cum when that cock of yours shows some progress in getting smaller."

The ice cold liquid caused the back rush of blood away from the tip of my now softening penis.

"There, now that's better. See how much quicker it gets soft, very good Henry, that is a little progress isn't it?"

I nodded as the Mistress patted my back in encouragement.

"Now put yourself back together"

I watched her as she wiped her hands on the towel she now threw to the ground at my feet. Turning she made her way to the door of the room never looking back more concerned with her mobile phone and calling one of the lovers she had taken then whatever I was up to. My only task left was to put the cage back on.

Glancing over I saw what putting myself together was made up of, the ring and the cage with the pegs and then of course the lock. The ring felt tight around my, what could only be described as my swollen balls. I say swollen, since Mistress has not allowed me to achieve an orgasm in almost two months now.

Once the ring was around both my balls and the now soft shaft of my cock, I had to admit they did have a slight color of blue. I tucked the shaft of my cock into the cage which in one click of a small padlock would encapsulate my cock with nothing more than a small slit to allow me to urinate through.

I often left stains on my panties as I was often leaking pre-cum throughout the day.

Mistress encouraged my feminization; well probably demanded would be a more appropriate description. Aside from the panties, my body was kept hairless, which I had to admit I rather liked but was loath to tell her about. I found it hard to believe that I was enjoying aspects of the transformation that was occurring, well up until then she began using that liquid on my cock, telling me that it was going to be a regular part of my routine that it would begin to shrink my penis. Evidently she felt that the smaller my cock was the more I would feel like a woman, or at least think less of wanting to play with it like a man.

I didn't believe her at first, but after the second application I noticed a tingling sensation, and before long I was having problems even getting an erection.

The tingling was in full tingle right now as I slid the pad lock through the hole in the chastity device. The panties I had been wearing were on the floor and I picked them up and slid them back up my legs, the slid easily because of the sheer thigh highs. They were crotch less-panties so the chastity device stuck through and was accessible, and yes they were pink.

I got up and left the room to find her. She was sitting by the bar talking to what sounded like Ricardo.

"Yes he can barely even get it up; I think I will see some better results in the next month or so."

She pointed to the ground and I knelt in front of her.

"Sure that would be great, I would love that, I know it makes me wet just thinking about it"

"Ok I will see you in a little bit then."

She laid the phone on the bar top and swiveling in the stool she sat in front of me with open legs.

"Stand Up"

I did this immediately, Mistress doesn't like to wait.

"I am glad you remembered, to put it through the hole for me."

Click…

It was done, nothing to do about it now she was once again in total control of its release.

The finger pointed down to the floor again.

I knelt.

"Seems I will be going out to Ricardo's house he has something to give me"

Her hand relaxed on my head tousling my hair.

"Now why don't you give a quick one with your tongue before I go."

She guided me between, knowing exactly where she wanted to have my tongue.

She always became wet when we had a session, the beatings she gave me were quite intensive, I really felt that she would one day actually orgasm from just causing me pain.

My tongue touched her outer lips, which were glistening and ran it up to flick her already swollen clit.

I began to work on her clit taking it into my mouth and wiggling my tongue back and forth and then up and down like I knew Mistress liked. It wasn't long before the pressure of her hands on my head increased, the scream that came next was filled with joy and pleasure and then her hands shook with a deep orgasm.

In took a few moments for Mistress to pull herself together but when she was ready she dismissed me.

It was a good thing too for I was way behind on the daily chores, just because Mistress wants to play with me doesn't relieve me from doing all my chores.

Stepping into the grey plaid skirt which was just long enough to come to the tops of my thigh high stockings I felt like such a naughty schoolgirl when Mistress let me wear that one. The bra was a good quality that snapped in the front which made it easier for me to get into, followed by the white blouse and plaid tie. I was still in my black heels, didn't really have a choice as they had locks on them and I could only get out of them when Mistress let me. It took me a long time to get used to the heels; I had them on night and day for two weeks before I had mastered them.

I touched up the make up on my face and super high glossed my red lips, and then it was back to the laundry.

"I am going out Henry, please make sure the chores are finished else you will be sleeping on the floor tonight. Do you understand?"

"Yes Mistress"

"Good, if you are a good boy I will bring you home a treat, would you like that?"

"Yes Mistress"

I watched as she closed the door departing to Ricardo's house I knew she would be having sex with him, that was the only reason she went to Ricardo's home.

I didn't waste any time but got back to doing the laundry, I could hear the click as my padlock bounced around as I squatted in my heels to get access to the dryer.

After the laundry it was to the kitchen and the dishes and then the moping, the afternoon passed into early evening when I heard the door open. Mistress was arriving home; I immediately put down what I was doing so that I could greet her.

I quickly got to my knees, looking up at her beautiful face.

"Put your eyes to the floor, who do you think you are?"

"I am nothing Mistress"

"That is correct you are nothing, you are a pathetic excuse for what used to be a man"

"But you have been rather good as of late, in fact you have done a good job being all you can be which isn't much"

"I have decided on a way to allow you to cum"

"Would you like that?"

"Oh yes Mistress, very much so"

"Well follow me"

Getting up from my knees I followed her to the back porch, she stepped out into the back yard and took out the necklace that held the key to my chastity belt, it was in fact the only key to my chastity belt as she had purposely bent and broke the spare key to show how important it was.

The key slid off the chain easily and fell to the palm of her hand.

"So here is how it will work"

I watched as she reached back and threw the key out into the yard somewhere, I was facing her so I couldn't see wear it went.

"When all of your chores are done and I have nothing for you to do, you can go out and look for the key, when you find it I will allow you to cum, and then throw it out there again."

"See now isn't that fair"

"Yes Mistress"

In reality I didn't think it was fair at all since my daily chores took me almost all day to do and then it would be hard to find in the dark, and we had a big back yard.

"Good, now why don't you get back on your knees and you can have your treat now."

"Seems Ricardo had a few friends over and well, let us just say they supersized your treat today"

I looked at her well fucked pussy and knew my treat the cum was deep inside and as I began to lick the cum up that was just loosely stuck to her crotch I could taste the salty creamy liquid mixed with her own. My tongue delved into her opening and I was further rewarded with quite a bit in one shot. It was so erotic to swallow cum from the men who had just fucked her, knowing my own load was building and building. I was sure I was already leaking into my panties leaving a wet spot.

I would have to finish up my chores quickly when I was done cleaning her so I could spend some time in my soon to be new favorite place, the backyard.

All I had to do was to find the key and she would let me orgasm, at least I had a fighting chance.

Of course if she didn't really throw it in the back yard, I was doomed to never be allowed to orgasm ever again.

And there I was…

My legs up in the air I was admiring my stockings and high heel shoes as I stroked my cock.

"You look so pretty with my stockings on, I guess you hadn't expected me home early from the office today did you." I heard her say.

"Did you think I didn't know about how you liked to dress up." She continued.

"I found your little pitiful cum stains on my panties when I was doing the wash over a year ago" She told me.

"You know sweetheart , you really you should have asked your doctor about why you can't cum like a real man" she said emasculating me further.

"You need to get those legs up in the air a little higher you perverted little freak" she commanded in a more harsh and demanding tone.

"Maybe I should tell you why I came home from the office early" she started

"I had taken a long lunch with your friend Bill, you remember Bill the one with the large cock" she stopped and let her words sink into me.

"I have to admit I wish I would have found out about your little sissy habits much sooner for then I would have made a move on Bill years ago" she continued.

"You must have seen his cock when you guys went to the gym, I mean how could you not have it is so big" she indicated with her hands a very sizeable cock size.

"Oh look you, you are confused" she said.

"I am talking about Bill's cock it is over ten inches long, and thick like a baseball bat, I couldn't believe it the first time I touched it honey, it felt so big and strong in my hands" once again indicating with her hands the girth of it.

"Yes that's right I touched your friends cock and I held it with both hands because it was that big, and I did more than that too" she told me.

"I bet you can't remember the last time I sucked on your pitiful cock do you" she asked?

"You should know that I was sucking Bill's cock today, started by kissing the head of his cock and then I rolled my lips down around it letting my tongue play with the underside until it was all nice and hard for me" she said with an evil grin on her face.

"It glistened, has your cock ever glistened, I mean other than when it is coated with pre-cum and covered by my silk panties" her jibe hit home with deadly accuracy.

"I had to admit I was a little taken back by Bill's cock, I mean I hadn't had anything that big in my mouth since college. It all came back to me though like it was yesterday, I took it slowly letting my jaw relax, keeping my hand at the base of his shaft to stay in control of it.   I slowly worked my mouth further and further down this manly shaft of meat. I worked my tongue underneath his head, oh he liked that a lot, I made your friend moan with pleasure" she smiled down at me.

"When was the last time you moaned with pleasure" she asked?

"Hell when was the last time you made me moan with pleasure" she demanded.

"His balls are about twice the size of yours as well, and I caressed them with my hand as I ran my tongue up and down each of them kissing them and I was lost in ecstasy just handling such a glorious tool." She said getting herself turned on.

"Of course I come home to this though" she indicated by pointing at me laying on the bed dressed in lingerie stockings and heels.

"Look at you wearing my thigh high stockings, my panties and bra. You are such a little sissy, and the fact that I am talking about cock has made your pathetic little dick hard" she pointed at my hard average size cock.

"Or is it something else that is making you so excited" she asked me.

"What is it that has you so hot and bothered; I mean I know you like playing dress up, you have even gotten kind of good at it and with your skin so smooth just like a girls" she was obviously getting excited.

"Could it be you are turned on by me talking about what I did with Bill, do you really like that?" she asked.

"Oh you are so disgusting, such a wimp of a husband, you should be angry with me for cheating on you, you should be going over there and demanding satisfaction from Bill" she laughed again.

"But you won't because you like it that I am taking control, you like it that I know about your sissy fetish, and that I am talking so sternly to you, don't you" she asked.

She pointed to the belt laying on the edge of the bed

"You see that belt there? I am going to redden your ass with it, and that is something I am going to do on a regular basis how do you like that" she asked me.

She proceeded to whip my ass until tears were in my eyes and the skin on my buttocks was a bright shade of red.

"I can't believe you, look at your ass now all bright red you look like a little school girl being punished in the principal's office. Well a little slutty school girl anyway." She said.

"Is that pre-cum on your cock" she asked me?

"I can't believe you are so pathetic, I read about this online, you want to be abused, you want me to control you and humiliate you, is that it." She asked me?

"Well let me tell you what else I did with Bill then, maybe you will cum from just hearing the words." She giggled.

"Since we were already back at his place, he picked me up and carried me back to his bedroom. He was a little reserved and he asked me about you" she said.

"I bet you can't guess what I told him?" she asked me?

"I told him the truth" she told me.

"I told him how your cock was small and that you had never gotten me off other than with your tongue, and I even went so far as to tell him how you like to dress up in my panties and stockings." She pointed at my throbbing cock.

"Guess you liked hearing that" she laughed.

"Oh Bill had a good laugh about that, and will probably be telling your other friends just what a pathetic sissy you really are, so don't plan on the usual banter next time you hang out with your buddies. " she told me.

"Who knows maybe they will pass you around and you can suck them all off." She said.

"Once Bill knew it was ok he took his still hard cock and rubbed it up down my pussy. God I was so wet for him, just sucking that cock made me ready for full penetration, of course I was used to your little penis, and

here was a man that the gods had blessed with a real piece, a real cock"
she grinned thinking back to the experience.

"Bill took it slowly at first making the head of his cock rub my clit which
almost put me over the edge itself I was already so turned on. Then, oh
my god, then he began to truly put that thing inside of me. It was like I
was being fucked by a fence pole. It hurt at first but it was the type of
hurt that you knew held a level of pleasure that was just over the ridge"
she said as she now sat next to me on the bed.

"Each time he withdrew his cock I knew a new storm was coming my way
as I felt his hips begin to move forward pushing cock deeper inside of me
each time it was such a rush to be so forcibly opened up in such a
pleasurable way" she actually moaned slightly when she was done talking.

"My legs were in the air very much like your own. My hands were on his
ass and I rode it down into me. I must have begun screaming after just a
few thrusts, but he kept coming down harder and faster into me. At one
point I was just hanging on for the ride, and boy what a ride it was, it was
like it went on and on for god knows how long. He just didn't stop or
didn't have to stop as he has some control, unlike you who if you stop for
a second your little cock goes soft again. No this was a manly man with a
tree for a cock and he was reaching places that had never been reached"
she finished but her hand was now under my ball sack poking around my
anus.

"When he was ready to cum I was in another world and he slid his cock
out and wrapped his hand around it and began in earnest to really pump
that piece of meat. I wasn't sure what to expect so I scooted down and
put my mouth right underneath the tip of that monster" she told me, and
she began applying some lubricant to my anus.

"He said here it comes, and I opened up and took the head of his cock
and began to suck, and boy was I rewarded with three or four loads of
cum, all I could do was to swallow then swallow again, take a breath and
go back to swallowing. One of Bill's loads is like having a meal it is so
big." She giggled.

"Did you like hearing about my day honey" she asked me?

I nodded my head

"Yes you did evidently. This is the longest your cock has been hard in
years" she indicated.

"I want you to know that I think you being a little sissy husband is a great
idea, you don't have to hide it anymore, I have already told all my friends
about what you do, and I told Bill it was ok to pass it along to your
friends too. I even put in a call to your boss so he knows just what kind

of person he has available to him. Oh don't worry he isn't going to fire you, but you may have some private meetings with him in the future." She told me.

"So from now on you will wear panties, bra's and stockings all the time, even at work, your boss wanted to make sure of that" she told me.

"I have another treat for you, I am going to take my fist and I am going to fuck you with it since Bills cock is about the size of my arm anyway so you should get some idea on what I experienced today" she smiled at me.

I felt her slide one finger into my ass and then a second finger soon she was she was up to four. What came next was one of the most intense feelings of my life. She tucked her thumb into her hand and began to push and then pulled back and then pushed again using more pressure, it wasn't very long until I felt the pinnacle of the width of her hand and then she was in and the waves of pain and pleasure coursed through my body, I wasn't even jerking my cock anymore but with each removal of her fist and then the reinsertion of it I found myself holding my cock pointed at my face and one, two, three times it was pulsating load after load of cum into my mouth and onto my face.

"Well I am impressed again longest erection and most cum I have ever seen you shoot, guess your penetration will have to be a regular thing after this" She told me.

She withdrew her hand and I jumped from the feeling of emptiness.

"I am going to go get cleaned up why don't you put on one of my dresses and meet me in the living room and we can watch some television and later you can lick my pussy and make me cum like my lesbian lover, and tomorrow we can see about getting me some more big cock." She said.

Then I watched her saunter away all the while I was thinking which dress I should put on.

A Note from the Author

Well here it is the end of another project, I get mixed feelings when I come to the end of a project, I enjoy writing so much that I am sad to be at the end but at the same time I know that now others will get a chance to experience my wonderful lustful and sometimes sadistic thoughts. I just have so much fun writing about the experiences I have with my own submissive play things, they are such good little boi's all dressed so pretty and they do whatever I ask of them, well they know they will be punished if they don't.

So now it is your turn to once again do what I ask of you.

I would like to hear from you, I am going to give you my personal email address so you can contact me so that I can get your feedback on the stories and the assignments and anything else you would like to tell me about. I would love to hear about your own stories and experiences, I just love it when I get email from the people who read my work, so don't hesitate to contact me, who knows maybe I will give you a special assignment just for you.

Write to me soon……..I always write back….

Love

Mistress Jessica

Mistressjessica01@gmail.com

www.ingramcontent.com/pod-product-compliance
Lightning Source LLC
Chambersburg PA
CBHW072301260726
48658CB00002BA/944